TIN CAN TOURIST

TIN CAN TOURIST

SCOTT HIGHTOWER

FORDHAM UNIVERSITY PRESS
New York • 2001

Library of Congress Cataloging-in-Publication Data

Hightower, Scott.
Tin can tourist / Scott Hightower.— 1st ed.
p. cm.
ISBN 0-8232-2151-2 — ISBN 0-8232-2152-0 (pbk.)
I. Title.
PS3608.I37 T56 2001
811′.6—dc21 2001040638

Printed in the United States of America
01 02 03 04 05 5 4 3 2 1
First Edition

For Nelda and Bill

Who shall deliver me from the body of this death?

Romans 7:24

Contents

Acknowledgments xi
Cemetery on the Ranch 1
Revelations 3
Easter Service 4
Graffiti 5
Commodity 6
Tenant and Outsider 7
Blades 8
The Showing of the Instruments 10
Triptych 12
Roman Remainder 14
Wedding 15
Cenote Near the Incarnate Word Campus 17
Lament 20
Burgled 21
Saratoga Gala: "Fearful Symmetries" 22
Six O'clock in the Afternoon, Las Vegas 24
Idyll of the Sero-negative 25
Andromeda 26

The Application of Force 27
Jefferson's Favorite 29
Love 31
At Toledo 32
The Taste of Sacrifice 33
Physician's Heart 35
Hujar's *Candy Darling* 36
Late Spring, 1983 37
Prometheus Saga 39
"Un Chant d'Amour" 41
A World without Art 43
Hart's Choice 45
James Dean 47
Rome '97 48
February Patience 50
"Bohemian Life in a Wicked City" 52
The Buddhas of Bamiyan 53
Tin Can Tourist 54
McCarthy Square 64
Kariye Encryption 66
Aboard the *Marco Polo* 67
In Medias Res 69
The Protestant 70
Executor's Last Resort 76
Trastevere Tesserae 79

Acknowledgments

Grateful acknowledgement is made to the editors of the following magazines, in which these poems first appeared, sometimes in earlier versions: "Idyll of the Sero-negative" in *Agni;* "Andromeda" in *American Letters & Commentary;* "Physician's Heart" in *Apalachee Quarterly;* "*In Medias Res*" in *Bay Windows;* "Revelations" and "Trastevere Tessrae" in *Barrow Street;* "Graffiti" in *Columbia, A Magazine of Poetry and Prose;* "Hart's Choice" and "Late Spring, 1983" in *The Journal;* "Un Chant d'Amour" in *Minnesota Review;* "Cemetery on the Ranch" in *New England Review;* "The Taste of Sacrifice," "A World without Art," and "Tenant and Outsider" in *Paris Review;* "The Showing of the Instruments," "The Application of Force," "Roman Remainder," "At Toledo," and "Burgled" in *Salmagundi;* "Lament" in *Southwest Review;* "James Dean" in *Yale Review.*

TIN CAN TOURIST

Cemetery on the Ranch

In time I would become the reluctant
heir to a brand in the shape of a fish.

But earlier, my older sister and brother
and I—having treatied up
our snarls—would tote hammers
and nails, and goat the gnarled climb:
part parsed and terraced fine black loam,
part brambled chert and caliche ridge.

All three of us climbed mindful of
the mounds in the valley just below
where the Tonkawa buried their dead.

If we took the climb in summer heat,
waves would wrinkle the distant
landscape; in winter, the view was one
of everything dormant in mourning.

And then there was the thing
that had given us our trek.
We pondered the melting
inscriptions: here, a skewered heart;
here, a last stand. Was hers
the earliest? The boldest?
Wasn't he our kin?

We used to come here
at dusk to catch fireflies.

We smeared their luminous oil
on our faces like war paint.

I step off into a pasture
full of summer flowers.

One day, I will lie among them,
murmuring of how the cedars,
broomweeds, and prickly pear
seem to be invading the countryside.

Revelations

My enterprising ancestors brought
salvaged notions of property
and capital, the Bible, and family names.
On the Virginia shores,

they were soon among
the Americans who turned
their taste from tea. No original testament
or personal manifest has survived.

One lone court record
of a judgment predates
early probate lists of household objects
and acreage on the Rappahannock.

The names and birth dates of slaves
also appear. A deed for Carey is interlined:
"and her increase," twice, before assigned.
Frank is noted "a mulatto."

One probate lists "four
horses, one small book,
a ladle, seven sealed
jugs of vinegar, and a skep."

Easter Service

1956, spring, rural central Texas:
a purpling sky clouding
like the curves of an unfurling
and downy, dark spring martin wing;
a rapid of clouds, mud-rose and changing.

This morning, the radio stays off
while we dress up like the pictures at Sunday school
stored in the closet beneath the yellow
pine stairs, the ones that lead up
from the annex to the baptistry,
that half-glassed grave vat that guarantees
every member sight of a new one's rising up.

This morning, my brother, sister, and I
improvise ourselves in sandals, towels,
and sheets. None of us is dressed as beautifully
as that picture of Him—blond, bearded, and crowned.
Or that one of Him painfully praying.

We step from our parked car
and, with the others, climb
the glowing, rocky slope
up toward the morning star
and three stubborn crosses that crest the hill.
Someone's heavy maroon velvet curtain
lies on the ground.

                    Metaphor
will dog me for the rest of my life.

Graffiti

Embarrassing sexual violence,
adolescence, the dew;
diabolically speaking—

the garden and then the tomb.
What betrays the magic of a kiss,
outlines a hand in red, or ferries

the messages of breath and blood
across to another's time? The torchlit
pleasures of play in untidy caves

are adorned with
Been There. Summoned
or *Survived This. Loved.*

Commodity

Here when I see
the huge, intricate, stationary crane
                    move the dull
          gray, rectangular, metal
containers from
ship to stack and stack to truck or train-car bed,
                    I think not only
          of the blocks and tackles
that I saw
used in Kerla and in Quintana Roo
                    but also of
          the ones we used on the ranch
when it was cold
(hog-killing weather) to lift the sledded bodies.
                    In that old clump
                    of live oak trees, they were hoisted
up, lowered down
into scalding water, and hoisted up again.
                    Here the simple
          instruction is everywhere;
on plate glass doors,
embossed in gold and silver foil cigarette package
                    liners. Now almost
          everything clearly packed
for freshness reads, "Pull."

Tenant and Outsider

No crisp white swans glide
conventionally across
the mortared, mud room shower's
utilitarian cinder block walls.

Along with mirroring gray paper ponds
and stenciled lilies, the trumpeting bravura
of swans remains relegated to the green, tubbed
bathroom at the other end of the house.

Here, the translucent plastic curtain
is grasshopper green, and, should I
finally get around to handing it
in to him, the requested bar of soap.

My gaze loiters;
laps at his pale pecan,
Mediterranean skin
glinting through the bubbles.

The swirling, soapy lather
burns in the drain
the way a white flower
burns on a riverbank.

Blades
(For Tony Kushner)

Now, sometimes, I go back down
in rodeo season and sit on the bleachers
among members of the community
where I was—as they say down there—
raised like a turkey. Few of them remember
who founded the rodeo.
                                        But many among them
still like to tell the story of the time my father
scored Gary Owens' horse's tail. Gary
was seventeen and, like all teenage cowboys,
fancied himself a full-grown man.

Their telling always ends on the tailgate after
the finals evening with B.B. cutting the cold melon
old-cowboy style with the same unwashed knife.
Almost always it finally notes him
handing Gary a half-moon of the melon
and Gary balking with always the same question,
"Berley, is that the same knife you used earlier
to thin my horse's tail?" At that the old-timers
like to drop their heads, arch their backs a little,
and thrash their thighs. It's storytelling body language;
everyone down there understands it. There is
a double pleasure in the story's catching both
the young and old together off their guard.

The story never makes mention that I was sitting
there and heard and saw clearly for myself

my father's purple-mooned nails
and the leathery backside of his hand.

It never makes mention of Gary a few years later as
a young newly married man (the marriage would not last
nor be his only one) trying to make a living as a butcher
in Stephenville and nearly slicing up his hand.

It never includes that I studied at one of the leading
universities of the nation. Or anything of the day
I was arrested taking part in a mass act
of civil disobedience. Of how, that day
in the snow, we formed a circle when we realized
they were going to take us; of how we tenderly
collapsed into one another looking up
at all the elegantly dressed office workers
that came to the great windows of the tall buildings
surrounding us to see what would happen.

A moment of calm and stillness
descended. We moved in tighter,
as if we could protect our edges.

The Showing of the Instruments

(*St. Lawrence Before Valerianus*,
Fra Angelico, ca. 1447)

There are all those scenes of pagan
administrators sitting before a wall
of patterned fabric stretched between
those pink, leafy pilasters of opulence
presiding judiciously over
the showing of the instruments;

those apparatuses, a tactic within a tactic,
usually lying on the pale ground
somewhere between the seat of authority
and the heretical stand;

solemn apparatuses of wood and iron,
a kind of static profanity
spilled out on the ground,
dark, symmetrical, opaque.

Never do the eyes of anyone
seem to move across them.
No, not their eyes. Only their
willful tongues and ears make clear
what truly is at stake.

This is the dialogue of intentions,
the display:

on one hand, the pride of ingenuity
of the torture devised;
diffused, multiple, and polyvalent;
as if to say,

"We can tear you to shreds
in the blink of an eye";
on the other hand, bloodless courage of
the accused whose instrument
in the investigation is the soul.

The gesture here is the juncture
between the judgment of men
and the judgment of God.

One will die without any doubt. Left and right.
In and out. Our bodies are our witness.
It is our soul that one must save.

We judge ourselves.

Triptych

Someone anticipates a buyer for the tacky
silver lamé evening dress. I wonder
If; Who?And then there would be shoes!
in my perusing the Bronx window, answering
the glamour of the canopy and sunlight.

No signs in the window display:
Riddle of Death, Riddle of Suffering . . .
Loneliness reduced! Fashionable Lovelessness
reflecting vanity, pride, stylized violence.

Ten minutes to kill till my friend's funeral . . . .

A flight above the canopy showers bread crusts
down to the bright sidewalk and my feet
embedded temporarily like a statue
surrounded by the jutting slate of hungry birds.

*

Throughout much of the service, my eyes rest
on an oddly kneeling plaster lamb in a holiday
creche. This is the house that Alpha and Omega,
Beginnings and Ends, have built; appropriated
Roman basilica, medieval incense, Oriental bells.
Sweet young poet: Irish American, and queer.
A companion, straight and Jewish, reads eloquently.

The acolytes wear black capes with shiny
yellow fringe. There's a word for such a garment.
When I was a boy, I used to wish for a vest
and matching pair of chaps with that same yellow
fringe. The priest's white scapular is embroidered
with a scarlet cross encircled by a scarlet crown.

Love does not envy . . . bears all things,
believes all things, endures all things.

*

Once delicious melancholy could be
infused into a posture. But now mourning
almost endlessly sweeps the garden and watches
the overlapping shingles on the house of grief.

Coming home with bags of groceries, I stop,
rest, and feed the birds. I quote scripture
to them, the one about the lilies of the field
and of the birds who don't stock up in barns;
drift in my admiration for their freedom
from self-pity. As I can't warn them about
the norther expected sometime later in the week,
I tramp home and gently heel the door shut.

Sixteen stories down and half a city block
over, dog owners frolic with their pooches
in the bright white beyond leafless trees. Brueghel.
Across the way, a black cross of emptiness
floats over a snow-surrounded air shaft.
One of my boots leaks onto a blond square
of floor. The blood-warming puddles of light
are receding. Forget the switch. Let the darkness
come. My waning strength is just one wing
of a frantic shadow slicing cold air.

Roman Remainder

I drift here on the bed alone—these are
the hours of revenge—a question mark, *Art*
Nouveau. My arms and hands are problematic.
My heart, once the size

Of a pea, has cherviled out. Trimmed, it has become
a support stave—with a pot atop to keep
from puncturing any tarpaulin. Stone.
A basket overflowing

with acanthus. A column with a cap.
A flock of birds. At first, your eyes
were travelers dipping, then lingering at a well.
Your hoisted brow

dispelled your daze, a torpid haze burned off
a bank or a façade. I lie here, still
a tongue; a surrendered ear listening
to the dunks and lifts

of the risen world. I am ash floating on your
rebellious reflection, the darkness on your
tongue, a faint torquated paraph,
a wing, a shadow.

Wedding

Like the night a tall
abandoned electric fan
slightly tilting in a vacant lot,
the wind gigging its way
through the whirling blades.

Another guest, a woman, already in
tears sits between us and the window
of the martyrdom of St. Boniface.

Menacing dark limbs
of an oak that fails to protect
sprawl across the top of the glass.

Eye of the storm, no hedging your bets.
His assassin is bare-chested.

The Frisian chieftain's swaddled legs
are crisscrossed up to the knees
with wide ribbons of orange leather.
A great atavistic hide on top of his head
cascades behind his neck and shoulders.
A leather strap runs diagonally
across his chest. A deep
crimson glass rag falls from one hip.

The barbarian clenches a short, wide
sword in his raised hand. In his left,

he clutches the bottom of Winfrith's
beard like a hateful valentine,
"Kiss it all goodbye, Boniface."

In his homily, the presiding priest
—young, clean-shaven, and condescending—
mindful of the absent, shares
his rehearsal gift with all of us:
a Navajo wedding basket
with an incomplete red
band ringing the bottom of the bowl.
Room for the spirit, the deliberate
crack in the circle is a way in.
'Til death do us part.

Rarely, if ever, has an age's
intension resisted the mark
of a mournful afternoon's
celebrated, ruffled gown.

By the jocular cutting of the cake,
the grimy hem of the buoyant newlywed's
lovely train heralds news of a mother
that can no longer be mercifully delayed:

Without a word, women from all over
the pavillion are hastily rising up
and moving to attend the bride.

Cenote Near the Incarnate Word Campus

Yesterday, all night, and even
now, one of the headwaters
of the bull-faced San Antonio River
continuously springs cold and crystal clear.

Both of my boots stand in a small nest
of tossed clothes. There are drawers,
and hangers in the closet; but a gentle
disruption may be what visiting
affords us all. A haze has crept in
like a great white sea cow that has
beached herself on us to sun.

Barefoot, past the art and the great
amethyst geode in the hall
I've accepted this window's quiet
invitation.
                    Virgil referred to it as
the undispersed pall of pallid fog.

Later, he lamented, "calves in the fields,
amid abundant grass, are dying on all sides
. . . yet the stock remains immortal . . . .
How often in the past the putrid blood
Of slaughtered cattle has engendered bees."

We all fear a little
the harshness of a hard season.

*

The world unfinished, where poetry still
has power: green Proteus drawn by a team
of three-legged fish-tailed horses.

The world in ruins: Aristaeus loud in complaint,
astounded by his mother's watery realms,
immured in dark caverns and resonant groves,
in daze of the mighty motion of waters,
source of all water which first has to flow
through fertile farmland to join the dark blue sea.

Orpheus in that moment of dark ecstasy,
Stretching to you, no longer yours, these hands,
These helpless hands . . .
he vainly grasped at shadows
With so much more to say . . . ;
am borne away
wrapped in an endless night . . .

*

Under the same chilly stars

but wrapped in the science of my generation,
I wonder if Virgil believed
that putrifying meat generated bees?

Bees hate carrion, even the corpses of the colony.
With other debris, they throw them out of the hive.

Does it matter that a farmer sacrifices
one of the herd and ends up with a musical
nest of contiguous, carnivorous wasps?

*

The fog today is as white . . . as—
no one who knows anything about milk
would ever strike such a simile . . .
as cold, purling water.

Lament

These are not the same orange leaves,
not the same water. Though the door
is open both day and night, these are not
the same black cattle grazing
near the land the living never pass.
Dead moon trumpets, dried
and withered, wrinkle in the clay.

The whole world seems to rush
with tears and mourn aloud.

Not far from here, I have sprinkled
my brother's ashes. Once, approaching sleep,
we helped each other wind our heads
with elm leaves, honeysuckle, and lilacs.

The falling water purls, "Go back.
For now, you need your comfort
and your heart."

Burgled

One feels the trail of clues is already
cooling: the abandoned highway,
the borrowed coach beyond its usefulness,
several smoldering trestles and ruined boats.
Everywhere the unexpected press
and violation of our polite but unsecured
borders, the helter-skelter of the plunder:
surgery, chemotherapy and radiation.
Still, the unstymied occupation,
and the butchered and abducted
for which not even love can pay ransom.

Few who can handle the irascible
deployment of hounds persist on
to the edge of the narrow lake, the melting
ease and difficulty of abstractions
dutifully refined and transferred: will;
the rugged, lamming to forgiveness and grace;
the road, now strewn with the litter
of someone else's body-gone-saboteur.
We study footprints, speculate how they
are drawing inevitably to the great gates
of a city, a narrow gangplank; what science
calls *the rate limiting step*, the shill
of corruption weaning
from the dance; the beloved,

withdrawing, somewhere preparing,
like a passenger boarding,

the rocking, the lift, the glide

Saratoga Gala: "Fearful Symmetries"

I say: a flower! and . . . there arises musically . . .
the one absent from every bouquet.

Stéphane Mallarmé, "Crisis in Poetry"

Familiar painted faces leap
across the blood-lit jewel-box stage.
John Adams and Peter Martins
are lost up on the sparkling July hill.

Beneath the grassy Adirondack
slope, a pair of principals glides
from step to solo point . . . and back.
She leans; he lifts her. A random pair

of classy words gleaned from the day
drifts out and weaves across the stage:
"disembogue" and "dogsbody,"
as if someone had furniture to move
or something to fetch—a picnic basket bulging
with candlesticks, a tablecloth of lamé.

Jezebel painted her face and sat
at her window. After her eunuchs
and the dogs, all that was left
were her skull, the palms
of her hands, the soles of her feet.

Like the music, the dancers
are fearless in their art.

Before my friends and I head
into town for drinks at the Adelphi,
a pair from the company—dressed
down and scrubbed—and I exchange
a kiss. A bouquet of flowers
that none of us know the names for
modestly adorns someone's gaudy table.

Six O'clock in the Afternoon, Las Vegas

> Into the wine of which they were drinking she cast a medicine of heartease, free of gall, to make one forget all sorrows. . . .
>
> *The Odyssey,* Bk. IV, l.220–21

Poolside at Caesar's Palace:
a mother-of-pearl sky,
several palms, and three
yellow construction
cranes hover over us.
The three of us—far from
our industries and grief—
are happy with our amenities,
"Here in the desert, fortune
will give you a taste
and then take it away."

Above what actually
used to be fragile
meadows, cohorts
of gold bulbs glitter
in the distance, "Mirage."

Idyll of the Sero-negative

We roll the dice and, in the twinkling
of an eye, the sharp blade of diagnosis
separates us from the clean lambs

of sacrifice. We await the next
reported case of frenzied HIV cells
ensconced in CD4 lymphocytes.

You describe for me what you sometimes
come across in your journals, photographs
taken through electron microscopes

of T cells infected with HIV. You evoke
the close-up of a head of lettuce
covered with bright, round blood ticks;

the curdled surface of a cauliflower
riddled with a parasitic caviar;
a floret of broccoli enlarged to an exotic,

satellite-grainy landscape freckled
with toxic poppies. The T cells and HIV
are closely matched combatants

like Enkidu and Gilgamesh, who made
the doorposts tremble and the walls shake;
who, together, in the forest tore out

all of Humbaba's insides, beginnning
with his tongue. *Death is our shepherd.*
Like sheep, we shall be laid in the grave.

Andromeda

For the sessile specter, a veil of spiraling
mist welds every intaglio carved by shadow.

The monster's forbidding carcass has already
washed ashore; its dazzling skin, dried

and flaked away like stony petals,
tears of relief, glyphs of an old sorrow.

The evening of the first harp, a light
wind blows across the beach. The sacred

ribs, picked clean and trembling, emit
only praise. On a balcony, something

in the listener stings as when her hand
draws cold water from a fragile bowl.

The Application of Force
(*Die Geisselung Christi,* Adriaen van der Werff, 1710)

I.

The officiously swathed governor
clean-handed, shaved, and crowned,
(insidiously unswayed) looks down
from the brink of a balustrade.

Knout, Bull Pizzle, a *Skinning Cat*:
though the family of whips is vast,
all serve a specific end.
The slender ropes of some,
at first glance, seem harmless;
at least here there are no sharp iron stars.

The post is low and squat,
not quite wrist-high.
Here, some have watched
while others have been whipped
into shape, down, up, to a pulp,
been beaten to a slump.

We can see how,
in the hollow of his lower back,
just above his naked cheeks,
his sloping wrists have been hitched
to the obliging column.

This keeps him, bowing slightly,
tethered in the well of spin.

Central to all of this
is the man
laved in the solution of constant surveillance,
unable to see himself as he is seen;
his expressive body,
stripped, in the light,
beneath the demonstrative blows
of this impressive,
arm-raised, backlit executioner.

II.

Each day the sun; everywhere the stars,
except in places such as this.
It is as if this day God whistled
and all of his luxurious dynasties of bees
immediately withdrew;
obediently abandoned the land.

Here one can almost feel
the field tremble, the earth quake,
hear Saul amidst the hungry uttering
"Withdraw your hand."

Jefferson's Favorite

> Above all things those of van der Werff affected me the most. His picture of Sarah delivering Hagar to Abraham is delicious. I would have agreed to have been Abraham. . . .
>
> Thomas Jefferson

> . . . and dream of freedom in his slave's embrace.
>
> Thomas Moore

Though, compositionally,
he is slightly higher, they face each other
almost eye-to-eye.
Their shoulders and palms provide a kind
of balance. At the end
of his extended forearm his right hand
opens and hovers;
his fingertips spread into the light.
Sarai's graceful left arm
arches downward, her floating hand and fingers
extend bright against
the darker den of fabric. As Abram
turns toward Sarai, his face
is dark with shadow.

The young woman kneels
on one knee before
the older woman who bows
slightly at the waist. Toward

the center of the canvas, the figures
echo each other.
Hagar's white left arm burns
in the light. Her fingers
rest on her inner thigh with a drape. From
our perspective,
it covers her modesty. Sarai's
shoulder and arm
are covered with cloth down to her hand,
caught between
the only choice (as he sees it) which
she can offer: her servant
or nothingness. Both women mirror
Abram's pose; each,
in the moment, reaches to shield her heart.

Hagar's left shoulder, upper arm,
armpit, breast, her side and belly complement
Abram's naked
right shoulder, upper arm, armpit, chest,
his side and belly. Alike
in shadow and in nakedness, their bodies
are separated
in the painting only by wisps of
her hair falling between her
shoulder and his side. Her hair falls tenderly
down into the rich
voluminous cloth which cascades
over Abram's legs
and lap, and across that brightly lit,
precarious bed.

Love

We never sleep apart—neither under
the stars, nor under a ceiling. Neither
"Staying over," up north; nor, down south,
"Spending the night."

We have connived our way through the streets
of old villages and new cities, have fought
our way through. Undress. Raise your eyes.
Forget about equities

and consents. Tonight again we are secure
as saddlebags astride the spotted rump
of an Appaloosa. Let surrender surround
as an unarmed Moor

awaits in his tent his enemy's cadaver.
Allow night to vault the fatal arrival
of such passing glamour. Forgive my lag,
my hoist. Raise your eyes.

At Toledo

From the balcony of our room, we watch languorously
as someone's untaken-in laundry hangs damp
and limp in the foreground of the light morning
fog like an angel's wing.

Our love feels scoured and clean. Today we will
not need the citadel, the martyrs' crowns or palms,
or any pair of green clad angels turning
like an effortless wheel

above a tireless executioner's elegance.
Happy that—at least for another day—
we've been allowed to wear the anachronistic
red robe of declared love.

As each one of our simplistic inventions
collapses under the weight of its own
pointlessness, we—like that concerto of hands
around Maurice's blue

cuirass—retire to the more complex obligation.
The gray wing tip only seems to brush the torch's
white rising flame if we senselessly discount
Depth. I adore you.

Close the shutters. For just an hour, forget
the Crisis of '98; the handsome corpse, saints,
monks, priests, gentlemen, the inward
procession of fire and ash.

The Taste of Sacrifice
(*Sacrifice of Abraham*, 1603; Uffizi)

There is no longer just the knife, a bundle
of sticks, and a pot with fire.
Other things have made their appearance.
A young stranger appeals to Abraham; has
already stayed his hand,
the right one with the glinting knife.
The boy no longer needs fear Abraham's
ecstatic precision. (Though
the patriarch turns away, his thumb
still presses sharply into Isaac's hollow cheek.)

No registry note relays
to us any of Barberini's
insight into the nature of Caravaggio's
imagination.
We can only guess. Had he
the chance, his paymaster might have
recorded three consecutive
payments for Andy Warhol's straddling
(six-shooter drawn) *Elvis*, emerging like a
giant. No, to original sin.
No, to final salvation. No, to . . .
innocence. The figures here, Hibbard coyly notes,
"are linked more intimately
than in some of his earlier paintings."

Here, we have Caravaggio parrying
in the game of signs; Cardinal

Barberini paradoxically
imploding in his fashionable generation's
violent and destructive
systems of interpretation. Traps
within a trap. "There is no longer just the knife,
a bundle of sticks." Three payments
for a metaphor. "A pot with fire."
Three payments for Caravaggio's interpretation
of a myth; one we
recognize to be both as real
and as fanatic as a dark massing of birds.

Physician's Heart

While you are off cutting people's rib cages
open and courageously massaging hearts,
I sit here and fuss over my spare diet;

sparagmos (a ritualistic dismemberment)
and *omophagy* (the ritual eating of raw flesh)—
my *Webster's Third* fails me;

rending, tearing, scattering;
and my penchant for trichotomizing:
haughty, inflexible, superstitious. I love you

for your virtues. Life is valuable. "The heart,"
you say, composed, "isn't filled with passion."
"Seen any seats of misery,

anger, or bewilderment?" I ask.
I will confess, sometimes, while working
over a tight column of verse

about cures and maladies,
I have a vain impulse
to tear its side and let it bleed.

HUJAR'S *CANDY DARLING*
(*Candy Darling*, Peter Hujar, 1974)

The glow of an upturned hospital sconce
and seven white chrysanthemums;
you are 28, an unusual age
                    for bone cancer.

Six years have past since your cameo in *Flesh.*
(Hollywood eluded you;
                    Midnight Cowboy.)

Tonight, a rose lies with you in your bed.
Its leaves and stem are a black sprawl
draped above the abject elegance.
(There is a faint descant
                    of ticking.)

The features of your painted face
float like fascinating pools
on the pale surface of gentle
and undemonstrative glamour:
polite, remote, curving,
                    compositionally exact,

no gaudy jewelry crumbles off you.
Only your thin hospital bracelet
links so willowy a form
to what even those among us
who do not know the story
                    can't help seeing,

the inevitable short stay ahead.

Late Spring, 1983

For Kary Mullis*

The mysterious interactive properties
of that delicate strand, the car snaking along
the moonlit road, and the quaint and probing
mind meandering inventively in one moment
became aligned: passage, edging

as carefully as a tightrope walker along
the rung between sense and anti-sense.
The inventor's thoughts accelerated
through sequences, reiterative loops,
hunches, and precarious calculations.

The product of (the reckless white stalks
of flowering buckeye) one cycle (where
the redwoods start) would become the
template of the next in a chain reaction.

Now we widely copy the delicate chain
with a technique of conceptual simplicity
(one that lay unrecognized for years
after all the elements for its implementation
were available) unrecognized until
a moonlit drive through the mountains
of Mendocino County, California. Driving

---

* Discoverer of the *Polymerase Chain Reaction*, a laboratory technique that allows the amplification of DNA so that enough genetic material can be produced for experimentation.

as if in a position one could hold forever;
transfixed, but not like Daphne or Narcissus,
not by anything ahead or in the rearview mirror;
but purely in the requited, unbreathable depths
of physical unrest, expressions, nonetheless,
of dying fall in the soul.

The darkness pulled up like draperies.
And then, that transforming glimpse:

Orpheus and Eurydice,
Psyche and Cupid,
David and Goliath,
Elizabeth and Mary,
Jesus and John,

Guanine and Cytosine,
Adenine and Thymine,
Sense and Anti-sense;
stranded
in a position
they could hold
forever.

Prometheus Saga
(Oskar Kokoschka, triptych, 1950)

A gap of song in the tempest of a great desert:
a pair of forearms and entwining hands
emerge from the sandy oblivion.

*

A harsh modesty becomes one of the figures.
She curves down, intrepid. Like a washed
landscape, her form extends,
a valance of leaves. She reaches
toward a piece of fruit.

His shins—before a sky-drape—
corner a space: a square;
                    matches
   the one
her uplifted arms
form around her face.
A sickle of moon
wanes green from blue.
Unbridled horses
                    (one white,
  one black)
rhyme;
      canter free.

A yellow flower opens
over a few ripe grains of wild cereal
and the small eddy of one's own death.

*

Beyond the yellow and white
gulf of the bright fire,
a raging pack of specters
colonizes a bank
across the chasm.

*

Each morning, the sun rises
over a surface of chains;
breaks across hungry topaz
feathers: *What's done cannot be undone.*
I too, rather than be enslaved by another's,
must find my own order.

"Un Chant d'Amour"
(David Wojnarowicz, 1954–1992)

Even before you
                    —at the movies,
at the Fire House—
felt dizzy
when a pirate plunged his saber
through the body of another pirate;

before your Xerox collage
of Madonna and child,
                    Colt revolver in hand;

before those acrylic,
white curtains being sucked in
and out of that bold, black,
circuit-like, open window,
                    yield of your own
self-governed imagination;

                              wild flowers
were blooming in your blood;
                    were lifting you
toward the weight
of the pre-invented world;
toward your own radical gestures;

and, not only
(as you had feared)
toward us,
perfecting our rituals of death,

but also
(as you had hoped)
toward friends, lovers, and strangers;

to a politically charged
demonstration parade and fire.

Your photograph
of a Washington, D.C. diorama,
of buffalo vaulting off a cliff,
burned as an elegy
in the middle
of a busy Village street.

A World without Art

Today I had a postcard from a friend
traveling the other coast—how pleasant
the modest arabesque, the unsolicited
thought and script, the self-expense.

At first, I thought (upside down) it was
a basic sky-blue Idaho. Turns out to be
San Francisco and the sky wedging down
between the Palace of Fine Arts and a corner
of one of the figure-graced garden boxes
atop its colonnade, 1915.

Over its Corinthian-capped (from this
angle, calliope-like) columns, from one
of the round portico's broken plinths,
a statue beckons.

Four draped muses emerge to the coordinates
from a swirling curtain of acanthus leaves.

Atop the flanking colonnade are empty boxes.
All their corners are attended by a grieving woman
whose shoulders extend akimbo. These,
with her upper arms, slope out to rest
on the top of the empty skyward planter.
Her hands fold back into her lowered face.
The card implies that she is only one of many:

"The weeping women that grace the Palace
of Fine Arts' colonnade were conceived,
according to their sculptor, to express
the melancholy of life without art."

I will tack it up on my condiment shelf in my kitchen
with the bannered, neatly rowed corn fields of Iowa,
Michelangelo's "Bearded Slave," and Siena's Il Palio.

Hart's Choice

"... this cup may not pass away except I drink it ...."

Matthew 26:42

In 1929, Crane wrote in a letter
to Waldo Frank:

"I've already seen a great deal—
tramping around by myself,
drinking Australian wine
with old charwomen in Bedford Street—
talking with ex-soldiers,
and then the National Gallery
with its marvelous
Agony in the Garden of El Greco."

*

For the companions, watch and sleep
have become one event with the angel:
spiraling, summoned cupbearer

of bitterest decision. Half-spread
sails involve the clouds.
The cloak-like rock,

a gesture of nature's protection,
shapes an echo, almost
an envelope, fragile illusion.

A flowering insufficient sympathy
surrounds the spreading arms
—wave against wave: the final prayer.

James Dean

"One crowded hour of . . . life [being] worth an
age without a name."

" 'The Lord is my shepherd.
He maketh me to lie down in green pastures.'
My mother died on me
when I was nine years old.
What does she expect me to do?
Do it all alone?": the snipping
with each coaxing of the Scissors Dance.
The healthy Bachir circling,
"It is always green and cool. . . . ,"
and the rigid Michel giving in.

Left of Dick Davalos—on the set
of *East of Eden*, in a scene
the studio censors would not let
Kazan include in the final cut.
Literally, Cal piping
the destruction of the old
morality by atavistic capitalism.

Actually, Dean, "fretful and uncertain.
God, he gave everything he had."

Rome '97

Via Veneto, once the site of the odd opulence
of La Dolce Vita, and Via Sistina gently slope
into the Piazza Barberini. Now, in season,
tour buses set down here. Their guides carefully
mark attention to the fountaining marble
   trumpeter held up by the tails of fishes.
Among other's, Richelieu's great emissaries
fretting over Sweden, the Huguenots, and Spain,
may have once primped or keened their wits here
before ascending to their mark.
                                                        Pilgrims
now shuffle off to the stones of the Spanish Steps
or the stores of Condotti. Others will sacrifice their
single day—Tivoli, San Pietro in Vincoli, Trastevere—
for a place in line for their ticket to the newly
cleaned murals of the famous papal chapel.
Until today, they've only read about them
in newspapers or seen them in photographs.

Rome can be very hot in the afternoon. Some
young men ambling in the Borghese Garden
take off their shirts.

                                   Having wound our way back,
early evening, we set off from the square
to the nearby Palazzo Barberini. First, towering
Herculean Hermes of the fence and gate,
and a sculpted crest: three bees below crossed

keys and a papal crown. Then, a rattling palm
and an expansive face of palace windows
looks down on us. Beneath our feet, gravel
crunches. Rome is hot. The famous stairs inside
are cloaked and scaffolded. A colorful wallboard
with elaborate diagrams and cross sections
explains the stages of how the once elegant palazzo
will be restored. We can come back in official hours
to view an exhibition of paintings. This evening
we wander along the driveway through the palace
arches. Statues adorn niches; most are dusted
with a layer of dirt. A large part of the ground floor
is a portico. A little deeper, on either side of us,
a pair of dark curling stairs sweeps up. Out back,
twilight begins. Beyond a crude wire gate,
a warren of rabbits scurry across the palazzo's
rear, shadowy, tree-crowned, side-garden
lawn to munch on lettuce and oranges.

Back out front, sitting on the edge of the dry
entrance fountain, we dredge up what little we know,
and admire the lasting beauty of the building's
design. We resolve on our next visit that we will
come earlier, bring our camera, take pictures.

February Patience

In the vestibule outside our mailroom,
neighbors grumble. An overhead light
reflects in the dark, polished granite floor.
The smug and elitist require a patience.

At least twice,
Emerson was recorded
to have opened the coffin
of loved ones

Each Valentine's Day I give my lover
roses. I'm that kind of guy.

to gaze upon
the corruption time had visited.

Three images from someone
scroll through my mind,
the ache of sensuality, the ennoblement
of love, the taste of raspberries and cream.

Thoreau
was
arrested
by his own image
in the river.

The notion of domestic and international
mail as a vigilance wells up like a gift.

I repress saying, "Patience! My father was
a rural mail delivery man. He drove
his backroad rounds even in nasty
weather; keeping current information
about each household was his business."

We can only
feel ourselves in
opposition,
sense ourselves along,
surmise from random reflections,

Three blue hydrangeas on the stamp
of a letter lure me to the news of a friend's
loss. "Three weeks ago," the letter says.

We can only
behold the ancestor
or loved friend laid to rest,
the shimmering
moon in the shivering river.

"Bohemian Life in a Wicked City"
(For E. B.)

In one of today's postcards, Sally, a character
from a novel, sits beneath a window,
cigarette holder in hand, green nail polish.

On the other side, the cost of the stamp
is inscribed above stiff-looking ends
of an angel's colorful wing.

The postmark rings
and encircles a smudged arc
and the last two digits of the year.

Two lines in the legend
are underlined in blue:
". . . Whose moral values

were crumbling under the pressure
of the impending chaos of oppression."
A frame of slashes sets off our address

above the overflow of scribbles
and capital x's and o's. Our friend concludes
with her stylish generosity and bravado,

". . . Love, stay well, and buy many tables!"

The Buddhas of Bamiyan

through the harsh surrounding landscape
into the beautiful valley of the peaceful buddhas
they, for centuries, have stood at the crossroads
of several sweeping moments in history
their niches in the sheer cliffs
a remote part of reaching destinations

they stand in the stone—
abhaya-mudra (gesture of reassurance
                    made by the right hand)
vara-mudra (gesture of dispensing favors
                    made by the left)—

now we know
they are not there

they stand gesturing in the *mihrab*
where any submits
his malice and intolerance

they were standing in the stone
before they were teased out
by Gandharan chisels
before the plasterers' drapes of lime and straw
before the painters' red and blue
before the brushes of gold

they stand in their porches,
in the shadowed arches of the stone

Tin Can Tourist

Boy, nothing in art talks like a human skull.
Randall Jarrell

When my modest and pious grandparents
traveled and bought postcards of places
like Pikes Peak, Yosemite Park, the Royal Gorge,
what exactly were they after; what
did they need to remember, and exactly
what was it they needed to forget?
The once pristine, white sidebars
of what were their cattleguard and ranch gate
now stand rusted yellow and streaked like horn.

Odd—to me, now—that they never flew.
Never absorbed the aerial advantage
that I've grown used to.
My grandmother—everywhere she went—
carried stale sticks of chewing gum.
She always issued them in halves.
(A complicated woman, that one.)
He was polite, diligent, and clean;
kept Folgers coffee-can spittoons
beside his reading chair and under
the driver's seat. I occasionally
joined them. Once—a big journey—
we drove his sister home to Bakersfield,
California. It was oven hot. That summer,

we abandoned our central Texas fishfries
and deer trails to "see the USA in
a Chevrolet!" from their finned white Impala
(red interior; tail lights that glowed
like little space-age stainedglass windows).
Seven of us packed in: my mother,
almost-grown sister, brother,
the two of them, and *his* ancient sister.

WHAT was *he* thinking! Whatever;
his example for me that trip was
that of artful packing and the juggle
of gentility, eccentricity, and responsibility.

Painting, postcard, poem,
delight of the garden, foreign vista?
What is it *I* am after?

*

Two postcards, gravures of interiors.
Round windows tucked deep in vaults:
Chartres & Notre Dame.

I also peruse the great high windows
of Westminster Abbey and St. Michael's
of Linlithgow. The spires of Kingston, New York;
Greenville, South Carolina; and Topeka, Kansas.
The modest geometry of the porch and window
of Little Flower Church, Hollywood, Florida.
Sacred places and inner windows everywhere!
And here, a turn-of-the-century set
of black and whites of someone's day
at the dilapidated mission of San Diego.

*

Some bottles and stamps, according to their color,
were redeemable. The first day of school,
we knew we were important. Most recent
from the great pool. Ignorant, awkward, and pure.

It was clear that we were special. We were
lined up and shepherded everywhere.
The shiny long hallway floor
ran the entire length of the building:
first grade on one end, twelfth on the other.
We were looking at twelve long years.
No crime. The shiny floors didn't smell
exactly like lemons. This was our day
to get a taste. And we were special.
Next year, there would be lockers
and days I would elect to play at recess
alone. I laid together limestone rocks
that were strewn about the playground.
Memorized borders. And I collected
pieces of broken glass. Arranged them
by color. And festooned the ledges
of the little limestone structures.

Years later, these bright Texas days
tucked away and forgotten,
I would visit the oddly familiar
mosaicked ruins of Pompeii.

*

Starlight, star bright,
manifest in me what I see
in some women who wear colorful,
artfully constructed clothes,

and in other women who have
absolutely nothing to do with the shifts

of fashion or seasons. Bring me
such . . . self-possession.

Bring me efficiency
like that of the great human
invention: the sentence;
vital and elegant in its simplicity.

*

gem red doors and blue sky
the gloaming the vanishing line
people in line to cash their checks
like wall mosaics of another empire
where processions of saints pass
in file with crowns of glory in their hands

*

Some restless nights I have elected
to walk amid the neon signs that blaze on,
even after the bright copulas of the city
have reached their appointed hour
and switched off. Mailmen are delivering
correspondence in their dreams.
All of the letters are in beautiful
ancient yellow envelopes, each
with a red and white, burgundy,
navy blue, or deep brown stamp
canceled with circles and waves.

My great-grandmother raised peonies.
Both my grandmothers grew lovely roses.
The one who lived out on a ranch
far from almost anything, had bushes
and a modest trellis at the end of her house.

*

Pocahontas, Joan of Arc, and a black Madonna
appear dwarfed by Lottie Moon. Beautiful mosaics
of martyrs. Kids frolic in a country swimming hole.

In a corresponding panel, a large
public pool is teaming with pleasure
and lots of radiant poolside posing.
A diver hangs in mid-dive. Others wait in line,
their backs to us. Some of the lads wear old
full-body, wool swim suits; and some,
waist trunks. What's caught here is a specific
moment of changing time. A mother leans down
and chucks the chin of what seems to be her child.
In another, young women drape and coil themselves
around a ritzy hotel pool admiring the physique
of a handsome "no one kicks sand in my face" guy.
Glass umbrellas. And here is a beach somewhere
in the 1800's. It's an unairconditioned summer
in . . . Galveston, Biarritz, Laguna Beach?

There are high-minded panels.
Elizabeth Bishop of the east
corresponding with Richard Hugo
in the west. Whitman with a ferry
in his lap and Crane with a harp
that looks like the Brooklyn Bridge.
Emily Dickinson and H.D.,
each holding white daffodils.
Marie Ponsot speaking with one
of her juniors. Both with sapphire eyes.
The glass artists have given him red shoes.

And then there are the darker panels.
Bullfight, cockfight, fishing,
falconry: vestiges of the hunt. War.

Animals and humans killed
by the simplicity of exposure.
Cliff pueblos, burial mounds,

An odd one of deer carcasses
hanging in mid-butchery.
Lovely fish glittering in the sun.
And disturbingly placed panels
of men in feather-decorated war bonnets;
a lovely manicured retired slave market;
a synagogue. A garish street of neon
and glyphed signage in some city's China Town.
A hauntingly lit opalescent gallows;
a baguette-emerald, sterile
gas chamber; a topaz electric chair.

*

Two postcards, gravures of interiors. Light
streaming in from windows onto stone
colonnades and wooden benches.

St. John's Chapel in the White Tower;
the Tower of London.

And the Auditorium of Calvin in Geneva.
Stern dimensions,

disciplined yet graceful.

*

List and turn: fuss and noodle.

*

a post to hitch
for water and to gather
or dispatch news

convenience
officious point
on a courier network

a local can dispatch
correspondence
or be delivered to

the abstract
—fixed and real—
domain of sovereignty

identity
estate
and location

box to drop
box to check
box to change

once there was
a stagecoach   a trough
beautiful combination dials

on little glass windows
a station master and clerks
stone buildings   a flag

to mark the direction
of homesickness

*

It takes some source of light
to read a book at night.

*

I occasionally used to visit
the Copley Plaza Hotel in Boston
to engage their telephone. Once,
standing in an even incandescence,
I was told of the cut-glass jewelry that
women used to wear at night in the hotel
and of how it would glitter in the gas lights.

*

What exactly was it they needed to remember,
and exactly what was it that they needed to forget?

I was fortunate as a youth to stand
beside intelligent people as they admired
expansive views: cities, meandering gorges
cut by ancient rivers, sunset on a sea.

I've logged in *my* moments: Santorini,
Rome, Mahabaleshwar. Mendocino,
San Roque & Gibraltar. I've rafted
the Colorado. Visited Piazzali Michelangelo
& St. Minato del Monte, Santa Maria in Trastevere,
Trocadero Plaza, the Spanish Steps.
Watched the morning haze burn off the Indus.

Stood before some of the most beautiful paintings
in the world, admired dancers from standing-room-only
dives, pondered the façades of the library at Ephesus,
the Palazzo Barberini, the lovely baths of Ronda
and the thermal baths of Pompeii.

What exactly was it they needed to remember,
and exactly what was it that they needed to forget?

*

The stake, the chair, the chamber
is often painted with a convenient,
sulphur-yellow despairing light:

the extracting stake, the chair,
either spiked or electric,
the chamber of solvent gas.

It is something—but not
exactly—like separating
a metal from an ore;

or a little like treating
something with a solvent
to remove a sovereign

substance. It is a little
like burning the heart
out of an old stump;

best scorn free, clean
as a drug traditionally
extracted from a green vine,

a red flower, or orange bark;
one whose inner garment once
rustled upon being harvested

for relaxation or to dispel pain.

*

. . . after four days
of artful renunciation,
Lazarus responded; stepped out,
stared into his teacher's eyes,

and, from that day on, he was
called—and later written about
as—John.

*

Once—in an era teaming with propaganda
and coursing with the enthusiasm
of an adolescent—in a squiggly hand,

on paper that probably wouldn't even
make it into the next century,
someone wrote, "Sublime."

Starlight, star bright, bathing suit, swim suit,
when it comes to the things for my suit-
case, keep me buying less but better.

Lighter, lighter. Preserve in *me* the terror
and comfort of the vista, the erotic charge,
the agape of the swimming hole,

like the prized photograph going
chocolate or fading to amber
with a single word inked in its margin.

McCarthy Square
(Seventh Avenue and Waverly Place, NYC)

Further down the avenue,
red neon reads: "BAR
DIX ET SEPT," an intersection

that's seen some artful flirting,
riddle of loneliness, refinement
in the pursuit of pleasure

as ancient as sweet desserts
or the spy hole in the wall.
In the deep window, behind

where we pause, closed Venetian
blinds backdrop a pair of shadows
like chopsticks or knitting needles

spread akimbo. Somewhere
on the street, two lights
light one geisha doll.

No staccato hammers
nor zippers of saws, no bell tinkle
nor fragmented poetic duet.

A wig with a delicate decoration
like a miniature chandelier,
a silk chrysanthemum kimono,

and a training, brocade robe
covered with tiny fans
attire the doll. A real fan

in her hand almost covers
her made-up face. In the center
of the square, between us

and the distant red neon, light
and shadow cut around the sides
of a modest marble flagpole base:

"WWII: * Brave Men and Worthy *
Patriots Dear To * God and Famous *
To All Ages," grafts of the spirit

that survive our fake, our real,
our imaginary victories; our fake,
our real, our imaginary ruins.

Kariye Encryption

Odd, this "country" church hunkering
in one of Istanbul's quiet, sprawling suburbs.
Setting out, neither of us foresaw
standing under the Scroll of Heaven.
Our first impression was simply: Why
would a neat white conch be floating
on the ceiling of the *parecclesion*
of Chora Church? "If the good Lord is
willing and the creek don't rise . . . ." Today's
dependable book, *Lonely Planet, City Guide,*
only offered, "The frescoes appropriately deal
with the theme of death and resurrection."

This church's serving for four centuries
as a mosque, the fragile aspiration of our
order, and all our ballets of violence
are scrolled up. One great orange
moon & sun already emblazons the neat
white cylinder's spectacular closing swirl.

Aboard the *Marco Polo*

"Some contend that Jesus traveled earlier
in the mysterious northwestern lands of tin
with his great-uncle, Joseph of Arimathea."

Our deck chairs are comfortable and sturdy.

"Joseph, like an offering at a pagan altar
or a 'Jesus Saves' sign at a southern rural
junction, is—after all—one of the points
where all four of the gospels cross."
"Some believe that Mary found
her way from Ephesus to Marseilles."

Over the animated shoulder
of my unscripted deck-companion's
jacket, specks of light glimmer.

His graceful wife and a friend of mine
who have been off promenading together
glide down the stairs to our speculations
about historical turns and high heresies.

". . . *shekinah*. For the founding Christian
fathers, *any* notion of a historical bride
would have been rivalrous and disconcerting;
though each of us, willfully venturing,
dreams of pure love."
                    We abandon
our drifting Tyrrhenian conversation

for the pleasant chides and banter
of our *belovéds*. Lyrical sinopian stars
loop overhead where—to our delight,

tomorrow night, will be the orange
interruption of Stromboli's mouth.

In Medias Res

I am already inside you. But the dumb
fingers of each of my hands probe your armpits
as if looking for an orifice. My tongue
and lips have found one

of your feet, and already know what to do
with it and its toes. Tomorrow I must remember
to give you the word for it, "shrimping."
Be but foresworn . . . thyself.

Reach in beyond all ironies, all violence,
all panics. Feel the black wind on everything
beneath your naked face. Feel the water lifting
you up. Un-

lock. Believe in your own presence,
a lotus blooming like a syllable inside
your dark lungs. Let craft and passenger and
wind all groan as one.

The Protestant

. . . how well I remember . . . the reflections in the sleeping water. . . .

André Gide, *The Immoralist*

Odd, these maneuvers of righteous love.
The unique characteristic of the design
of zealotry is its single dark-paned
window and its narrow military door.
The sharp rhetoric of righteous indignation
comes from the curb, outside the rolling vehicle.
The earnest faces of a crowd of protesters
angry with the Lincoln Center screening
of the new movie, "Dogma," wad in belligerence
and malice; fill a policed-off corridor.

*

The papers, this week, have been covering
another controversy—over at the Brooklyn Museum.
Some political flap involving artistic
sensationalism and dung as a medium.
Years ago, when living in India—Colva,
Goa—I rented a room in a Portuguese bungalow
and spent a clear December day working
with the owner of the house, pouring kerosene
into tubs of fresh cow manure. The paste,
worked up and smoothed across the house's rough

concrete floor, dried to a clean thin cushion.
Underfoot it was as durable and satisfying as paper.

*

A turn of the "Ram Van" and the wave of the protesters
sinks back into one of the streets of the Upper West Side
of the city. This avenue still dissects the same
Hell's Kitchen streets which, in another time,
inspired Bernstein's *West Side Story*.

Behind the Lincoln Center Plaza fountain—
tonight, full of silhouettes—are the five
dramatic, high arches of the Opera House
and the two floating panels of Chagall.
Once in a theater, a doctor pressed a finger
into the dark gape at the back of Lincoln's head.
One night, in an Indian village I have long since
forgotten the name of, an English-speaking Hindu
vandal armed with a can of spray paint and wit
scripted out, "The Differences are Interesting,
But the Likenesses are More Important."
By the afternoon I encountered the clumsy
double clause, it was faded and had been patinaed
by the elements. Tonight, somewhere in this city
on the other side of the Enlightenment,
a graffiti artist sprays out another
cosmological note in wet paint:
"You can never have too much protection."

*

The walls of many old *New World* churches
are carved palimpsests of a layering.
The order of names listed on the wall
of one of the Catholic churches
of the Lower East Side of Manhattan

is distinctive: German, Irish, Italian, Chinese.
Outside, graffiti scrawls absolutely
declare there can be no substitutions
for the metaphysics of our senses,
no substitution for the poetry of our lives.

*

For a moment the silhouettes are medieval specters.
How the bloodless, gone voiceless
come back to us in unexpected guises.
As if the Lincoln Center subway entrance
were a gate to some heroic transport;
the yellow traffic light, a golden bough.

The dresses of German American women drowning—
a wet nightmare: their rings, the lockets of their necklaces,
bent and burnt, the dry cork in the useless 1904
USS *Slocum* doughnut floats and life vests;
the wheel of the burning vessel breaking bodies;
the picnic boat disaster of a Saturday afternoon
before Hell's Gate. The reports of Protestant disasters
almost always used to note the final hymn they sang.
Almost immediately, an entire Lower East Side
community of mourning men sought for
and found new wives in the upper 80's.
The exodus it led to changed, almost overnight,
the character of two Manhattan neighborhoods.

*

"If this were a conceptual poem, its title
would be scripted on a wall in neon blue:
You Can Never Have Too Much Protection."

"Garlic braids and umbrellas,"
your lips hover near the receiver.

I get out my thank you

for the exotic bouquet
of blue carrot tops shading up
from purple at their base: "Eryngium,"

spiny silver stars. My dictionary
notes its roots were once
ingredients of candied aphrodisiacs.

Are you revolving in your
un-airconditioned apartment
before a full length mirror,

your hairline freshly trimmed?
There it is: the familiar
rattle of ice in a morning glass.

Our shared pleasure of iced coffee
& exactitude seems ancient.
"What about poor Jupiter?"

"Sinking into oblivion,"
I mumble. "I need to go.
I have a lot to do.

Behave yourself . . . ." Honestly,
like a shameless bottle fly
drained by its profane paraphs,

I release the old envoy
of declared love. My cliché's
acceptance of its own responsibility

rolls predictably to stillness
in the geometry of your cul-de-sac.

*

When my job offer from Fordham came,
it was to Edgar Allan Poe I turned
for a character witness. He liked the fathers
of St. John's College, his neighbors.
He said they liked distilled spirits, were well read,
and could be engaged in friendly and first-rate
conversation. I wonder what they thought of him,
a writer out among the Fordham groves
of fruit trees and gabled cottages; a sickly
wife, a household dusted with poverty,
and a sweet hope at the bottom of his soul.
Top of a hill, the rented Poe Cottage nestled
in its cherry trees and greensward swatch.

The dusty roads, Catterina, the cat,
and the caged birds are gone.
The Fordham house is still there.

*

Tonight in Chelsea, steps
outside my door, a brief

chance encounter:
a friend and I exchange

a goodnight kiss. Just
last Friday, he lost

his home to fire. Odd,
it being one full year

since mine burned;
and, that—even as we speak—

his white blood cells
are chum to the shark.

Takes less than a second
to run a check,

detect an oasis
or a loaf in another's eye.

As emotional tenderness
goes, this is "high cotton."

A few steps later,
alone, standing

at a Mexican fast-food
counter, I admire

young Chinese
men modestly

performing their duties
like dancers in clear air.

*

there can be no substitutions
for the metaphysics of our senses,
no substitution for the poetry of our lives.

Executor's Last Resort

"... simple pleasures ... are the last refuge of the complex."

Oscar Wilde, *A Woman of No Importance*

The reputable estate ledger—insisting
upon compliance—is, after all,
for balancing the complex
with the ideal that dwells in the place.
Like a canoe. Volume to steady volume,
an evocative row—from Whitman
to Faulkner, the poems and stories,
no matter the weather or music.
Passion has been boiling up,
like a child vulcanizing for limits.
Every saddle-brown leather volume
of the ledger wants balance. Like
a canoe, shape of an inverted service cap.

The ledger is just the ledger. More often,
it's the passions of a family squall
that has me wishing for a remote place.
A camp reached only by canoe, a wattle,
a simple tent on a sharp, wooded bank;
a single story, a relaxing second floor
loggia, long and full of episodes.

How tempting to be triggered by the oversimplicity
of unhappy family members: Caliban

anxious, no matter what he sees in the glass.
Like roses, thorns are famously self-evident;
and, in their elegance, they lay their
undisputed claim to the complexity of the rose.
The spokes of fate spin on a wobbly axis.
Michelangelo, in his portrayal of the mysterious
realm between God and man wisely left a gap.

Love of the unmoved mover spans the bank
eventually to ricochet back. . . . B to A:
the distance from a Blake or an anxious Auden
back to an Abel. From the Eumenides,
fertility abundant and running all around,
back to the blood vengeance of a Cain.
The ache. Ancient frenzy, come to your
senses. Prosody. Come to the limit,
the last visit, the ledger,
the survey and land deed; to literacy
and the breathing gyre and script of the law.

I live far from the pastoral landscape
of my childhood. Walking to my job
in the Bronx, I pass a pathwork of shops
that resonates with decisions. The modern world
squares off with the ordeal of the wilderness;
and every day our humanity goes on trial,
a string of tests and choices.
Some legacies, once pressed into service,
limb off to a renunciation;
though the wobbly wheels of buying,
selling, and inheriting roll on. On my way
to work, I regularly see young soldiers wearing
garrison caps and shiny shoes. This afternoon,
two with flyers solicit outside the recruitment
center on Fordham Road: just up block
from the shop window displays
chocked full of cheap shoes, jewelry,

and gold talismans; a block
from where the cottage Poe rented used to sit
on the edge of the hill's ridge before it was moved
nearby to restoration and safety in a park;
just across the street and around the corner
from the cathedral-high Emigrant Savings Bank
with its five floating monochromatic murals
of Indians and pilgrims; just around the corner
from the deteriorating clock, a detail
on the façade of Loew's ornate Paradise.

Trastevere Tesserae

"Who, busied in his majesty, surveys
The singing masons building roofs of gold"

Shakespeare, *Henry V*, I.2

On deck, in a hot tub, sailing *from* Byzantium:
the Topkapi Palace grove nestles behind
the shrinking Hagia Sofia and Blue Mosque.
In Rome, the Ponte Roto already points her way,
Santa Maria in Trastevere with anachronistic palm.
Her pavement of porphyry and *verde antico*
spirals and circles between the nave columns.

These pillars once flanked Caracalla's
dome-topped caldarium, tepidarium,
great triple-vaulted frigidarium,
and the large natatio that opened to the sky.
Salvages. Citizenship, inheritance, taxes
extended by imperial decree. Though doomed
revetments of financial crisis and collapse,

the marble is still beautiful. Here,
heaven and the hill are even more abstract.
Two of our coins rattle down through the box
to light the high chancellery wall and dome.
A lion, an angel, an eagle, an ox: beautiful
tesserae. The mosaic band of thirteen sheep.
A caged bird. A ceiling radiant with gold.